PETALS AND THORNS

Ikechukwu Francis
Okoronkwo

Order this book online at www.trafford.com
or email orders@trafford.com

Most Trafford titles are also available at major online book retailers.

Print information available on the last page.

ISBN: 978-1-4907-7653-8 (sc)
ISBN: 978-1-4907-7652-1 (e)

Trafford rev.   08/27/2016

 www.trafford.com

North America & international
toll-free: 1 888 232 4444 (USA & Canada)
fax: 812 355 4082

Title: I Too, A Shoulder to Rest
Medium: Oil on Canvas
Year: 2004
Dimension: 36inches x 48inches

DEDICATION

For Magdalene and Mariana, who have taken petals to the land where the moon is the floor

Your songs still echo to the aerial zone.

PART ONE

(SONGS OF A COMMONER)

Title: I Too, Am Human
Medium: Coffee, dye and ink on paper
Year: 2001
Dimension: 16inches x 22inches

LETTER TO CHIEF I

Why did you send your son
Across seven hills and seven rivers
To learn the secret of signs and symbols?
With tarnished coins, you bought his way
To waltz with white lilies in ballroom floor
To cruise in Pathfinders and Hummer wagons?

But you dropped this killer machine on my hands.
You twisted my mind not to see beyond
The cloud of lies you stuffed in my brain.
Like a zombie, I turned the efficient AK 47
On my mother, on my father, on my brothers
So you continue laying wreaths on diamond streets?

I too am human,
I too am from your clan
Son of your kin, brother to your son

Your son, the prodigal has traveled with rented papers
And he flings our paper of value toward the aerial plain
Little did he know how many were killed or killed?
As he continue laying wreaths on diamond streets
So that billows of thunder will kill our clamour
So that we swallow the line you dangle before us?

Why did you send your daughter
Aboard the aerial plane to pluck
Those beautiful cherries from golden trees
And stretch her hand to touch God's house
And speak in the language of the alien King
And gather the peacock's plumage around her neck?

I too am human
I too am from your clan
Son of your kin, brother to your son

But, you rent out my sister's thigh to your friends
And blinded her eyes with nuisance notes
To celebrate her death on your vision of lies
And decorate her killer like a rich banquet table
While your daughter sits beside his Excellency's son
And continues to lay wreaths on diamond streets?
I will turn this monster-pump on you
So your eyes will drip blood…blood…blood
And water the seeds you have planted
So your son will come back to fight his war
And your daughter will feel the heat of many loins
So that our Christmas tree will glow for us all

For we too, are human
We too are from your clan
Children of your kin, and human

LETTER TO CHIEF II

Now that you have released
Your fart of repulsion
See! The wry dog cannot endure
The stinking mounds of dung
From your sickly entrails

You say again and again
That your blood runs blue
Your ordination is for ever
What again is remaining
From your royal thoughts to us?
Crooners will rehearse
A new song for the mercuric fluid
Of your kleptomaniac fingers

Do you wish to bless us with the loot
So we can sing praises of your royal fibers?
Royal fibers of nothingness
Or should the minstrel compose a new song
A disgraceful dirge
To haunt your shadows forever

Title: Stock of Illusion
Medium: Coffee, dye and ink on paper
Year: 2003
Dimension: 16inches x 22inches.

MERCHANTS OF ILLUSION

What happened to our vision of the aerial plane?
What happened to our dream of petal and roses?
What happened to our journey to the ethereal zone?
Where is the fire we all gathered wood to kindle?

What of the awaited sun we all expected?
That even my father's father begged to come?
Did it come and your massive form covered it?
Do you still peddle your illusion for us to buy?
Yes the fire burns just for you alone
And you give spillages to your obedient friends
And you told us it's wise to be your friend
After all to whom the sacred pear glistens
Let his pallets do the justice alone

But sir, look at the man in the mirror and ask
What happens to those hands that kindled the fire?
What becomes of those mouths that blew its ember?
What becomes of minstrel's sweet voice now sour?
And the choric contribution of us that gathered
Or have you sent all of them to voicemail
Where they will be locked forever

As you sell illusions
Have you exchanged your promises?
With new song of impertinence
Before our clamoring eyes
And say

What is mine is mine
What is ours is mine
What is yours is mine
What is mine is not yours
Even as your mirror image is us
With swollen eyes, blotted lips and spindly limbs

MISCARRIAGE

When this monster belches
Will it spew the bones of Mother *Odi*?
Will the flesh of burnt *Jesse* be thrown up?
What becomes of the mounds that now host *Vandikya*

The Atlantic
Because it is full
Has begun to vomit in Biafra
Regenerated flesh, bones and blood

When this multi-headed monster belch
Will the bones, blood and flesh
At *Ikeja* tell us to our faces
What we should have done but did not do
What we should have said but did not say
Will the bones of Biafran youths
Struggling to live again
Remind us of our miscarried justice?

THE POLITICIAN

His insanity has hovered airily and
Has filled up all the vacuum of our world
Even before the mother of all lies
Floats from his entrails
We know promises and realities
Dwell at opposite ends of our land
Yet some of us love masturbation

We gather
At the market square
With expectations
From our world of dreams
And he stands on a raised platform
An ominous figure of delusion
He borrowed smiles from Greek archaic sculptures
With flowing *Agbada* like insatiable oil barrel
And floated before our naked eyes
Binding our thoughts with veneer of naira
Buying our senses with cheap currency

Chuckling, he clutched and pushed his knuckles
The air around us paved way for him
His grotesque lips parted to release captive lies
All the winds rushed and captured us
Winds of deception contaminated us
We laughed, we chuckled, and we giggled

His voice filled our expectations
With borrowed dreams and painted promises
Reality in a hall of mirrors
There the myth of beginning diverge and converge
Then he massaged our wounds with spurious balms
I will make tars in your toilets
I will keep air conditioners in open field
I will plant gold on streets of diamonds
Your old and young shall hunger no more
Only touch your finger-prints on my portion
And hunger no more, clamour no more
As you take your trip to the cemetery"

Even this Shall Pass Away

A night of horror
A night of sin
Crawling mischievously
Children of the underworld sing to agree
An Owl hoots for the umpteenth time

Nocturnal beings chant
Their song of torment
But I will wake before the final sleep
Before these lids are glued forever
Before these limbs are locked forever
Before this lips are sealed forever

I know I will wake
The conundrum will lack its puzzle
My eyes shall pierce the secret of night
To pick a silver pin from the dark

Yes I will soon wake
I will surely wake to pluck my petals
And take my sit on the lofty row
Where favored children shall count my trophies

GOLGOTHA

At Golgotha
Bones of known heroes lie fallen
Skulls of unknown villains build mounds
Trees of truncated dreams grow new branches
So frightening and yet so enchanting

At the Golgotha
Where the moon turns blue
Songs of death dance through living spaces
Black roses grow towards the abyss
To bury the last life of a dream of life

At the Golgotha
Where the satire of end endorse beginning
There the renewal of new life starts
From the darkest sun of resentful death
And the remnants of cherished life
I see hint of real light rushing in

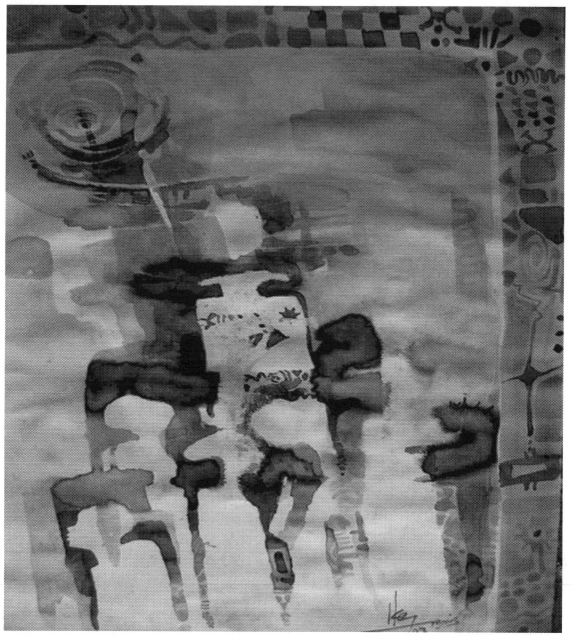

Title: A scroll of History
Medium: Coffee, dye and ink on paper
Year: 2003
Dimension: 16inches x 22inches

FORWARD TO THE PAST

Who heard the cock crow?
Again and again for the Alien king
Because our king slumbered
Tongue tied to his nostril

We all watched the she-goat labour in fetters
We all sang praises for the king's misdeeds.

Who will believe?
It is a sweet sensation
As the vengeful adder crawls
To take a kiss at the ankle.

We all watched the she-goat labour in fetters
We all sang praises for the king's misdeeds.

Who did not see the tinder
Glow at the diamond altar
While preacher-man in a cesspool
Recite an eleventh commandment?

We all watched the she-goat labour in fetters
We all sang praises for the king's misdeeds.

What shall we tell
Those children of tomorrow?
They are the untended tendrils
That crawls on the ground.

We all watched the she-goat labour in fetters
We all sang praises for the king's misdeeds..

Who heard the thunder roar
At the dying end of the crystal lightening,
Petals turn into thorns
And our young clutch the evil crown?

We all watched the she-goat labour in fetters
We all sang praises for the king's misdeeds.
Who did not see
The big children hold petals
With drips of our blood
They are rivulets of blood before us

We all watched the she-goat labour in fetters
We all sang praises for the king's misdeeds.

What hands did not hold
Those infested seedlings
Which have grown into giant *Iroko*
While we search for tubers among thorn?

We all watched the she-goat labour in fetters
We all sang praises for the king's misdeeds.

What eyes will not see us?
On that wooden cross of guilt
Where our silence
Has turned to many brushwood

We all watched the she-goat labour in fetters
We all sang praises for the king's misdeeds.

Who will endure the sight?
Of the forgotten nuisance rag
With all that we have rejected
Now our favoured costume for the fete

We all watched the she-goat labour in fetters
We all sang praises for the king's misdeeds.

What eye will say
It did not see our labour
Sprouted thorny weeds
At the season of harvest?

We all watched the she-goat labour in fetters
We all sang praises for the king's misdeeds.

ELEGY OF THE OIL GROUND

I am black
Dark, rich black
I keep treasures
Exploration and excavation has found me
In my bosom
Gold, liquid gold
Mysterious liquids of ambivalence

I am thick and darkly
Affable and impregnable

My black blood moves the world
My mystery liquid erects structures
Towards the aerial zone
People come from earth's end
To see through my magical bowel
My bowl holds people together

But I cry and I mourn because
Strangers turn my wealth to poison
And my people are lampooned
By the fist of privileged children
To push them to exhibit rags and rots
Sitting by road side to beg for food
When my bowl of treasures and magic
Enriches and feed others
Who build houses toward the aerial dais.

Title: See What We Have Done to the Earth
Medium: Coffee, dye and ink on paper
Year: 2001
Dimension: 16inches x 22inches.

BLACK GOLD

See our earth's floor
See our planet's base
See the hearth our elders sat on
There was peace when they met here
Then they palm wined with wisdom talk
But see today, see all the relics

See our beautiful woodland home
See our serene mangrove channel
See where our ancestors offered libation
Here they gave us the robust life we live
But see today, just see the devastation

See our clean waters
See our air of life
See where the deep water woman lived
Lived with her committee of friends
But now she is forced to flee
Away she has fled with her entourage
Our waters, no more dependable
See what they have done to our core

Here once stood big *iroko*
The tall tree that shaded us together
The totem of good value
The taboos of the old ways
Here also was the patched earth
Sipping endlessly from libations
Where our fathers circled with one heart
Yes there was one truth

But now, now the wicked fire pipe
Flaring the fires of disunity
And the tied brommstick is scattered
From Khana to Gokana
Blood runs like water that flow from well
Ogbe - Ijaw to Itshekiri sounds.... Clatter
Clatter, clang..... Clicks...... click.
Machete clash and blood flows
Oh scions of Jesse
In a macabre dance of cremation
Saved from the fowl of desecrated earth
Do you meet the ancestors in ashes?

Though the glare from the flare glows
Its dazzle is for others
Though the boom from the flare grows
It builds royal courts for others
But when it burns it heats our life
In our backyard our back is burnt
From the scourge we are baked black

And those promises of loving caress
Turn to a fatal backstab
The tree that flares wealth for others
Burns deep-deep our riches
The light in our backyard casts but only
Huge shadows of gloom,
Of degradation, of death
We have waited for the liquid gold
To light up our way
She has come as an eclipse
A thick dark mould...
... and my people
Host the black princess of death

THE DESTITUTE'S SONG

1

For these scavengers of national treasures
For these excavators of unnatural measures
For these imposers of cruel measures
And for these violators of moral cultures
I lay my soul bare so you can see
The several shades of suffering you create

Though I traverse through forests
And course through ochre and umber hills
To announce my unsolicited presence
I only live in the fringes of the golden city
Then you said I spoil the city's goldenness
I beg my way through to the periphery
You said I pollute the air in the city

From the edge without which the center dies
I cleave my claw like an agama on the wall
And swear not to come near your banquet parlor
Where you gather to scatter the loot of our treasure
Where piles of corrupt notes buy integrity
There you plunder and stuff
Then leave crumbs for your cronies
That allegiances be bought against me

2

You chopped my fingers
So I cannot print my desire on my life
You also sewed my tongue with strings
And caged all that I saw you do
You gorged my eyes that I see not your evils
Now I can't take my repressions to the Centre
Because you have chopped my fingers
You have stifled my voice
You have plucked my eyes
And you have told people, it is all I wish for

3

After you have made me an incoherent imbecile
You made yourself a buffoon
As you plead for a print from my chopped finger
I wonder if my rotting arms
Can draw graffiti of a fingerprint
To support your greed in a battle of thieves

I wonder if my rotting frame
Can throw punches at your fellow thieves
So you maintain your plundering of my land
My landscape where my creator deposited me

THE GENERAL AND HIS PSYCOPHANTS

My people, we go left
Yes sir!
No not left, we go right
Yes Sir!!
Ha! I think a little to the left
And a little to the right
Yes Sir!!!

Ohoo! I think something is not
Properly kept
Let us re-orientate ourselves
Democracy dem, all crazy
Ism – Skisms, mass hypnotizat…
Ye…e…ss..s Sir…r

Shut up let me finish
Sorry Sir,
Hypnotism, mobilization, orientation
Uumhh privatization, corruption
Now you did not answer
'-Ah, yes sir we waited for you to finish
Ah ha you spoilt the game at last
Let's go and sorrow
Sorrow for our indiscretion
We must learn a timely chorus
Or spoil our Zombie chants
Numbskull, rot and puss, sycophants
Eeh ehh putrescence of fart
Eeeh… just wait till I come again

ALIENS

Now we tread on thread
Of un-trodden road
Our path to fallow part
Experience in the virgin path
Where real turns to surreal
Head swallow whole

The story is unheard of history
Not their story but our unraveling story
This can-age, turning to carnage
Cyclops hobble from tubes of human cloning
Non-persons with borrowed limbs leap
Unto center with half-eye to lead
This age is on edge
Strangers strangle natives at dark ends
Strangers swing mallets in the market square
The new generations with borrowed genes
Without empathy or sympathy; antipathy
Is the story of strange people?

SONG OF AN ORPHAN

Machete kissed the cocoyam stalk
And in fright it quirked
Fire embraced the prawn
And in agony it recoiled

Let the stranger find his way in noonday
Through a footpath
Then search for the dark Billy-goat in daylight
Through yam-barns behind the homestead
For night comes to embrace it
Good *Nkwo* announces its brightness on *Afor* night
But the frail tendrils will build a fore-boding tuber

It is daylight now
It is still noonday
The secret whisper from mother to son
Is revealed to the orphan child by the mud wall
Even in desolation he learns the sage of life
His wounds will heal in due season
In time
By time

THE CONMAN

Here he comes again with his fat book
The good book with lines of life
Where he reads from the other side

Ha, please, please, please tell him
I will not go to his factory
Where he sells what he does have
It is for conmen and heartless people.

PART TWO

(SONGS OF THE MIND)

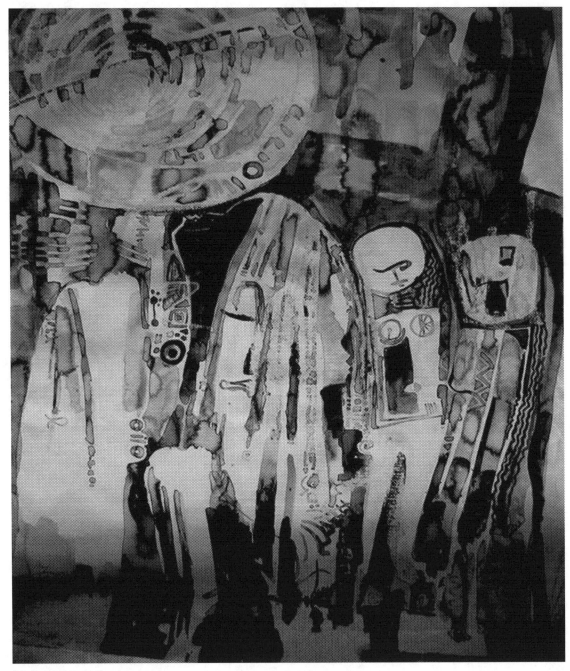

Title: A New Song
Medium: Coffee, dye and ink on paper
Year: 2003
Dimension: 18inches x 26inches

THE EAGLE PERCHED

The Eagle of beauty
Has perched on my heart
When my soul is yearning

The Eagle of beauty
Has landed on my heart
When my soul is fertile

The Eagle has brought with her
A seed from heaven
She will cultivate
In my vast farmland
For buds, petals and fruits
And we will dine with joy.

Mystic Bird

This exotic bird of mystic Eden
Has perched on my precious garden
Beautiful colors mark your quills
Dense and ready to kill

Your beak is red like burning fire
Your chest changes hue to spur my desire
Because you have rehearsed for a huge feat
As I am trailing your gallivanting feet

Though you have torn my soul to shreds
Pick the pyrrhic trophy if my blood is shed
Then perch on another garden so innocent
And whole, surround with your alluring scent

YOUR SHADOW

Like a patch of red on a green sea
You mounted my dormant soul
Flowing ceaselessly like the *ulasi*
To occupy my remote heart

Your shadow torments me
Your furtive shadow torments me
Your shadow fights my dreams
Your shadow is the hue of bird with plume
Your shadow appears like a flickering light
And I cannot stand your brazenness:
The spectacle of your plumage
As you dance *atilogu* on the walls of my soul

But I will quench your fire
To erase your niggling image forever
To dream new dreams of colourful petals
To hold my thoughts like pearls on my palm
Then your shadow disappears with the quenched light
The roadside foliage shall echo new songs
Of new testaments without old shadows

TEASER I

Why have you come to break
The horizontal restfulness of my sleep?
And yet cannot be bold enough
To announce your vertical growth

Why have you left an indelible print
On the plate of my heart?
And yet will not soothe it
With your magical touch?

Just let me be who I am
For my oil has not been refilled
The straw mat I had is shreds now
But never mind, it is threadbare
They do not bite or choke
Forgive me but just let me be
My powerful brother has taken my inheritance
He says I did not pour libation to grandfather
And the community cock will crow for him alone
But if you will decide to stay with me
Remember, the tidal wave has come to take me
Across the other side where the cock crows for all

II

Did your quivering arrow pierce my heart?
For you to remain unattainable
Did the gushing blood from my heart
Soften your tense muscles so you can smile
To assure your timid mind of your pranks

Or is this your game
That you have perfected
Pluck your cupid rod
From my heart
Or, I will drain
And your game will be over.

WILTING ROSE

Withered Roses
Garlands of yesterday's dreams
Litters of once-upon-a-time lust
Like a rumpled love letter
Burning with tears of pain

Now a scrap of ugliness
On retreating foliage
Where you violate the green splendour
Just yesterday you vowed to lift

See how rivulets of endless tears
Stalk your abandoned hopes
From bees who gild your nectar
Of dreams truncated before its wake

Pity you carried in your trail
Petals of a patched land
Of perforated lust and greed
To mount your rose on thorns

I Waited For You

You said you will visit me
To show me how you care
To bring me whispers of your love
To run those soft fingers on my spine
And to sooth my heart with your song
So I waited, and waited, and waited

You said you were in the green house
With pink hibiscus and purple roses
With petals from vanished flora
With garlands of an unknown banquet
And scents from an ancient vanilla
So I waited, and waited, and waited

You called to say you were delayed
By a traffic jam
By a sudden gust of endless rain
By a gathering whirlwind of dust
And that you would soon be with me
So I waited, and waited, and waited

I called your number to hear your golden voice
An unknown voice said your network was busy
A stranger said you were not available
An alien finger wrote "network failure"
And my life burnt with desires for you
So I waited, and waited, and waited

My door rocked from a push of an empty wind
The earth pounded but it was two dogs on heat
Love moans from two lover-birds rushed in
There were two pigeons on my rooftop
Shadows of you passed before me
But it was the coming of evening
I drifted into a sweet dream of you and me
But I saw you hand in hand with a stranger
Like those pigeons in deep kiss
I saw you in airtight embrace like those dogs
I also saw your purple roses and pink hibiscus
In fingers that were not mine
Then I knew I imagined you in my arms

CONTRADICTIONS

Oh! How I hate to love you
Because you make me cry

How I despise my feelings for you
Because you make me think I am erased

How I resent the jelly spot I kept for you
Because it tells me that I am spineless

But I will not love to hate you
Just because I hate to love you

Until I unravel the secret of the moonlight tale
Where we have gathered to build fantasy castles

Helpless me! I love you, I love you, I love you
Logical me! I hate you, I hate you, I hate you

I will sing it to the wind
That in turn brings back choruses

I will paste it on trees
So souls who shy from love will read

And feel my deepest contradictions
That I blindly live to defend

Yes! I hate you, I hate you, I hate you
I hate to see you loving me to hate you

I hate to feel you do things
To see me swim in the river of hate

For that which I think does not exist
For that which I believe is not me

I hate to see you cast my love away
For saturnine birds to peck endlessly
I hate to feel my love could stay
Without my love and be happy
So I love to love you erase the hate
And wake to see that love kills hate

THIRSTLES

Now you have me captive
By desires of inner me
Now you have me bound
With manacles crisscrossing my drive
Now you have me prisoner
From my wind of freedom

I follow your tormenting fetters
As your newest victim to the abattoir
To add to your mounting skulls
To surrender to you my Achilles heel
And be slaughtered by your feeble arms

Do you wish to stand by my tombstone?
Weeping rivers of tears for a pyrrhic prize
Or taste vinegar when you eat honey?
Would you love to stand barefoot
On shards of a broken self with tied hands
You cannot pick and patch your remnants?

Title: Grave Dance
Medium: Oil on Canvas
Year: 2002
Dimension: 48inches x 74inches

SEPARATED

If I could take
A trip to my antipode
I will see my muse
Seated as a sad minstrel
Singing me a dirge
Of my neglects

She will sing her cry
You have left me
For Awan, yes for Awan
I see only your back
As you look to Awan
Yet she turns to you her back

Your colours has turned pale
Because Awan has visited
Your muse gathers rust
And Awan dream of galaxies
To pluck stars from the sky
She is learning new dance steps

II

The Iku sings bitterly
You have brought an alien
To scare the first born
Pretending you have grown
Ahhh! I see this stranger
She is a butterfly turned into bird
A bird of exotic colours

Call the *Babalawo* for my friend
He is blind and cannot think
He is numb from an Adder's bite
He pretends he is living
He is pallid, he is sallow
His eyes are jaundiced
This General is pale from attack
Aaahh! I sense this stranger
The butterfly turns to a bird of colours.

III

I know my friend
The General of the hearts
Usman try to rationalize
Detour is his strategy
He will be back at the right time
His soldiers he will not loose
In this battle of the hearts

IV

Awongo is angry
For the brewer of *kon no mi*
Awongo wants to change
The beginning from the beginning
She crafted an infested prologue
A beginning that is full of maggots

Be a man, be the man she wails
The man we all knew
A warrior with many victories
The one with skulls in his barn
For a General does not sleep
From an amateur cut of a corporal

V

In times of yore lived I
With my muse, we mated
Our children were like the rainbow
She was inside of me
She was outside of me
My muse was my essence

Awan! What did you do to her?
Age long connection you disconnect
What basket of lies do you carry?
That pollutes a pure love

I see you in your dream
Floating with the stars
Leaving undone things to be done
Chewing an after taste of fantasy
Postponing reality for tomorrow
Awan, dream to wake to dream again
See the sun never stops for anyone
It is I who is violated, but
I will not live in Awan's dream
So that I will wake on my muse' chest
As the midwives' hand is weary
Waiting to deliver new seeds
From over-charged semen
My muse awaits my coming.

MY CO-TENANTS

Chei my co-tenants
Always together
Dis early morning
Una don begin kiss
Deh do wetin I for like begin

Na waooh!
Una comot togeda
Una enta together
Una sing una lovesong
Una talk una lovetalk
Na so, so lovin lovin

Last night na murmur, murmur
Because of una kpuru, kpuru
I no fit sleep at all
When e be only me sleep here
Abeg tek am sofri sofri
Make here reach all of us

Ehen you see?
Broom don begin follow enta
Like say new tenants wan come
Any way shaaa!
Mek una no forget
To join pay rent with me
As una don plenty scatter for ceiling
Landlord no go send pursue everybody

BLEACHED

You want to be white
I know
It is in your breath you fake
It is in *Esau's* skin, you disguise
It is in your voice, you twist
But you will be black

You want to deny black
I hear
You speak foreign tongues
But you cannot mask
Your ancestral voice
You cannot wash your blood
You cannot change your essence
The sun will contrast you
And you cannot be a stranger
In the homestead where your ancestors lived

A Nigger's Soul

Was it for the dark dungeon
Was it for the dark dungeon?
That trailed your travail
Was it for the cold chains?
That tied you?
Or

The fish that rots from its head
Or
Has fate dipped a soiled finger
Into our soup?
We all clog below the ladder
To form a massive base
For other people's height?

BREAK THE WALLS

Break the blade of incision
Tear down the ruthless decision
Tie the hands from further dissections
For humanity is against mutilation

My voice shall shatter this ancient wall
These lines will crack roads from its hall
And set free the virgins awaiting cut
To flee the gushes on this hut

This blade shall open no flesh
For my sister's virginity to be fresh
This blood shall flow no more
For we are not fighting a new war

Do not paint red over my memory
Less I see the blood drip on your history
Or your fingers like claws of the devil
Tainted by these revolting crafts of evil

LAMENT OF AN OBSCURE POET

Am I the oasis in the desert?
Travelers come and get life and I dry up
Am I the lone bird on the tree?
Singing new songs for others to relish
Am I the lonely fish in the sea?
Swimming against the current
Like Ocalan
Are my eyes tied to Turkey?
Do hints of pre-natal plan elude me?
That I just grope, stumble or fall
But yet moving
Moving blinding
Thinking without thinking
Hidden in the disappearing corner
Watching the fishes
Knifing through the waters
Creating ripples
Am I in a stagnant pool?
Dead sheet of water
Without even a wave
Am I unable to chatter
The rap chant of a griot
Or do I sing to dead tunes?
With unmelodic notes
When yearning souls await
The ravishing wail of the village soloist

CRIES OF A PSYCHO

Loved ones look at you with bleary eyes
Friends wait for their conclusions
Contradictions woven in the fabric of their mind
Belief and disbelieve at war for a pyrrhic trophy
The loser mourns for injustice of silence
And they are debating about my san
But 1! I cannot control these elements?
But I! The eye that sees spirits
Can't I see the gathering of human forms?
In their eye, I see confirmation of doubt
Of my insanity blossom

True, I reach the extreme of trials
Is it the friction before the stone is polished?
Is it a baptism of fire before the rite of passage?
But must I reach the extreme?
To pluck a diamond seed
At the cap of the tall *Iroko*

CONVERSATION WITH
MAGDALENE AND MARIANA

I would have died
Before Maggie did
So she wailed her life out
My son, my son
Do not violate Maggie
Child of my dream
Son of my peace
Petal of my joy
Emerunam Maggie
Do not bring thunders
To turn my waking joy
To rain of tears

My innocent spirit tormented
By Maggie's hot tears
My route became confusing
Red-tags on my recalcitrant spirit
So my young spirit be denied passage
Rivulets of Maggie's tears coursed
Through the canal
To water a gatekeepers path
To smear red patches on my visa
To swap Maggie with me
And leave me with three-quartre spirit
That I live from a three-quarter depth

At the orchid of scarlet petals
With trees that grows diamond leaves
Stood Mariana with palette of golden hues
A quarter from my three-quarter she took
That I live life from a two-quarter of one

Oh Mariana, Mariana, my friend, my friend
With my quarter heart across many waters
Through the beautiful gate as a gateman slumbered
That even my harangue was a meringue
Mariana passed unhindered

With my quarter heart and I with half
Where she fixed her petals on silver stalks
On the land where the moon was the floor
Where diamond bulbs grew on golden trees
There she went with my quarter spirit
My song were without melody
My words were without poetry

As she took her bag of rainbow to there
She turned back to me and said
Prajem ti vela sily, z ktorej buales
Ijit drakrat
I wish you enough strength
From which you will leave twice

BEYOND THE DIRGE [TRIBUTE TO MAGGIE]

Before the gathering of outcasts
On one leg I stood
Hooded in black
Black in mood and lonely I stood
Exchanging glances through hooded eyes
From ravenous eyes to abrasive minds
Though we were heart-miles away

Even though my heart bleeds
Not for exonerating tales we plead
Not the litanies of tales
The would-have-been that wouldn't be

The wouldn't be that have become

Draped me in black at the back-wood
I replayed from the antipodes of thoughts
Dreams shared yesterday with *Isikaoso*
Of tomorrow with boastful petals of roses
Today confused by a deafening thunder

But between shinning teeth dazzled hope
Of buds that are in gestation for morrow's flowers
Of light that opens the bud to plumage
As the thunder will yield new petals
For *Isikaoso's* dream will not melt into nothingness

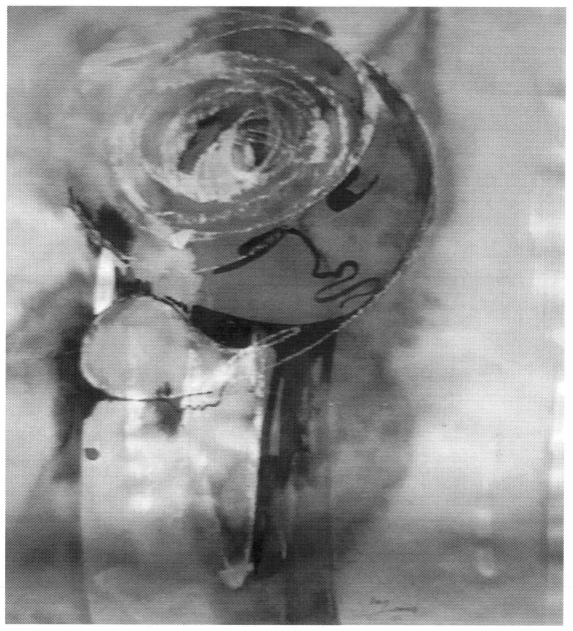

Title: Even This Shall Pass Away
Medium: Coffee, dye and ink on paper
Year: 2003
Dimension: 16inches x 22inches

PART THREE

(SCRIBBLES)

Title: Christmas Tree
Medium: Coffee, dye and ink on paper
Year: 2003
Dimension: 18inches x 22inches.

REMNISCENCE

This frigate coursed back
To distant past of yesteryears
Of my rich youth in a dim village
The nearby-cock echoed the time
From where I did not know
It came from far, far direction

I can only see my moonlike Tommy
Wooing the moon for a shining dance
Refracting the light to multiple glow
My playmates and me harmonizing the full moon
Challenging it with folktales

Also I hear echoes
The heartbeat of Africa
This night is clothed in mystery
Crossroads leading to endless crossways
And a web is before me

Now I hear the faint chirping
Of the crickets of the underworld
And the singing children of the night
Uche's tale of *Ogidiga* swims back
But this fluorescent pipe chases them away
And fireflies are now romantic tales
The dark rich continent is lost
This bright poor continent is in lust
Of shadows from distant land

SONG OF HOPE

It falls on every roof and shines
Sometimes the pond of affluence
Discriminates and settles only on
Those who are special friends with fate
Yes they smile
To the weeping of souls in penury
Because they only dream dreams of luxury

But there is a date for every player
Like a porker game
Reshuffling comes to turn the table
When the be will come to become
And these famished souls will laugh
When sun will shine their wretchedness away
And their toil will be rewarded.

HOPE II

Now when the moon is waning
The star is a mere reminiscence
A faraway memory forever
When the dark tunnel seems endless
The labyrinth keeps dark experience
And the shattered earthen pot is irreparable

At the horizon where all lines converge
A bright light will shine
Surrounded by hope and happiness
At the beginning of another testament
Devoid of foes and vendettas
And there we will see stars not mud.

ENDLESS QUEST

Exploration to where
Just don't know
But will continue to search
The nearer, the deeper
It is fate
It is strong
It is truth in a bottomless pit

REALITY

I was hit suddenly
From sweet retirement
To reality, I rose
To be confronted by reality
Wicked and unmerciful
The drive, the madness

My dreams
Producer and casts
I the sole producer and viewer
I labour and toil
Not like in dream
Not like phantasm

Reality is nude
Assertive and tenacious

NO. 19

In this dingy room
Water halves the tibia
Hurricane lamp tilts and sails
Certificates and papers float
Like colourful regatta at *Ogbuide*
Weak ceilings like pregnant cloud
Charge for a fatal release of deluge

From perforated rustic roof tops
Light peep as galaxies in the sky
Their grotesque eyes impishly watching
The bats passing through expressly
Through long forgotten shattered louvers
The smell of squalor
Surrounds the space at no 19
But landlord breaths hot air on my neck
With piercing words about
Rent increase! Increase!! Increase!!!.

DISVIRGINED

On this blank sheet I dance
Like an orphan child in a forest of life
My legs unaccustomed to its beat
My eyes still searching the faces
Until my arms grip its transience
The fleeting images my wet seamen will smear
Through a seriating pathway
Yet on this virgin forest I hoist my totem pole
To enter orgasm with shouts of joy
To live prints of my shaft in relief of dunes
And ease its placidity, its idleness, its void

With flowing dampness of ochre,
Of vermilion
Of yellow
To tell new tale of old faces with new hopes
Of eyes that reveal, that conceals inner events
Of lines that rise from nothing to serendipity
On this sheet I start the journey of experiences

TO THE HERO
(For Chike Aniakor)

He is a cat with nine lives
They tried to kill all
And frustratingly found out
They only shattered but
Eight mirrors that hosts the first
The first, their ninth married the wall
Nightmarish dreamers they were

He crossed the first river
A beast with seven heads appeared
Seven mirrors became his friends
The beast charged and raged
Seven beasts echoed rage
In ferocity the beast smashed
But the mirrors swallowed him
To shatter themselves

Then he crossed the second river
There *Ogumagala* appeared
That master of deception
Seven colours of spectrum
It bought over as allies
And they played sycophancy
So he borrowed a crystal stone
He reflected all with new dimension
And *Ogu-ma-gala* shied away

The third river was slippery
So he poured a drum - full of okra juice
He sailed in a dreamlike speed
And became a guest to over-side evil forest
There he passed out a stinking fart
That sent the fairies off dozing
Those little spirits slept for seven days
And he crossed the river of death

He appeared before the big *Iroko*
Just at the threshold of the fourth river
An old woman commanded her entourage
To bring him captive to wooly-hair- hag
They held him but he was a stone
They threw the stone at the *Iroko*
An easterly wind blew heavily
He shaded his weight and became wool
The wind carried him to the over-side shore
And the hag waited for seven moons

As the fifth river appeared before time
He released rivulets of spasm
The water goddess heard a war cry
And sucked all the waters to save her aquatic court
The floor was a patch soil of dried clay
He sailed thru before she realized her mistake
He looked back and saw the river rushing
With bitter and vengeful anger
And the mounds covered him from the tide.

At the entrance of the sixth river
Afor came claiming she is the mistress of the day
And must take him captive to royal court
He went and saw in *Afor's* rack
Installation of skulls of defeated heroes
Of tibia of adventurous youths
Of hearts of stillborn children
Afor turned to mud to mire
But he urinated into the mud
The stench suffocated *Afor*

The seventh river was an endless sea of waters
He peeked into his goatskin bag
His portion is spent save the coconut on his shoulder
He ransack the coconut thoroughly
And there he saw milk and honey
He remembered six rivers and six victories
He looked up towards the aerial plane
Where the princess stood with a crown
His head asked for the crown.

CYCLE

A full blown rose withered
The bud sings new song
Of yet to blossom petals
Butterflies hover around
Waiting for the next ripping
Maturation is on gestation
Tingling the eyes with visions
Of full season of colours
Colours of life full blown
Colours of life in transit
Cycle of joy
Cycle of tears
Boom, doom, boom, doom
A pink petal of rose spreads

In noonday with colours bright
In the evening it withered
Apex spells fear
Fear against doom
Fear for nothingness
While vultures flutter
Around waiting
Waiting for carcasses
To carry to craggy joints
Scarlet rose waits again
For time to shout again
And silent echoes of voices
Will respond the choruses
With refrains of multiple voices

CHALLENGE

Sun!
I will look at her face
I will see the dazzling shimmer
Of the ageless pretty maiden
The war of eye I will contest
To prove my manhood
For her enthralling beauty
The forger's hot iron I shall grip
With my bare palms
Ogun be my witness
My gritting teeth shall play tunes
For spasms of my muscles to dance
The footprints of my dance steps
Shall mark boundaries of the ritual grove
At the village centre where man and spirit gather

But I will cover my face with basket
Before the king and his faultlessness
I will dare to question his over reaches
Today shall bear witness to those
Perforated plates that hold his impeccability

If I see and see no more
And if I sing muffled with dust from earth
These voices have sang the soulful song
Of the weaver bird in a predator's cage
These hands have removed slag
From the forgers hot foundry
And have removed slag of royal imperfections

MASTURBATION

It is fantasy
I have been enjoying
I have clung to, like a leach
Sucking its juice of dreams
How pleasant your unreality
How despairing your truth
When reality cleared my eyes
To see your masturbatory bliss world

INCUBUS

I have traveled near and far
To where?
I do not know
Acquaintances
Fairies in a nether world
Unwilling pilgrims to abnormal terrain
The nexus…

There I am
Stifled self desire
For what essence?
I do not know
But I struggle
To control consciousness
I struggle
To live
Brother help me out of the nexus
Sister I need release
Jerk! Jerk!! Jerk!!!
I won't stay here, it's no home
No promise is good enough
No…
Are you just a dignified observer?
Watching me pass through life and death
And I shout without sound
I gesture without motion
Who can help me from?
Nexus, a strange place

ODE TO ORACLE

Not yesterday of foot prints to obese *Iroko*
Not the streams of redcap elders with goatskin bags
Running down from their shoulders with worries that sent them
Through shaded serpentine tracks to huge installation
The shrine your abode

Not the tremulous cry of the emissary
Between the oil bean to bread fruit trees
Nor the mystic echoes from *Dibia's Ogene*
Piercing a loud silence
Could open our eyes to know that your life is
A chameleon; changing with time and changing time
You dance to unfamiliar tunes
You sing your strange tunes
And we are blind, we are all sightless

To know that the milky way is a silver strand
To follow an unending tread to your wet abode
To see you shedding effete garment for new ones
Because we were blind, we were all blind
As *Nwokeke* wails with *Ogene* and *Konga*
Not even his piercing voice made sense to us
Ah we are blind, we are blind and deaf
No one knows the mouthpiece draped in leopards skin
We have covered our ears with fiber from borrowed cultures
We covered our eyes with films of floating reality
You traveled from across great rivers
As you split your soul to minuscule demons
And lives in matchboxes and big witch-boxes
For us to click the cowry for you to come

We are blind, we are all blind
Like the son who thinks he can have
A son before his father
And veils his sight with empty words
To forget where his umbilical was planted
Ah we are blind, we are too blind to see
To know that you traveled through golden bulrushes
To be adorned with royal garment by the children of others
Who love and respect you

To know that you are back to walk among us
And touch lofty corners of our expected dreams
To turn a twisted trunk
From patches of modeled history
Even so, welcome in your assumed guest-hood
At favoured rift-driven homes
In the bosom of our pockets
And in centers of our village square

SONG OF VICTORY

Blow the flute of *Ijele* blow
Let the minstrel play his tunes
My legs like the *Atilogu* dancer
Will dance your strange tunes
And dance to unsung melodies

Blow *Ijele* blow again for
I will dance here and beyond
Even the king of dance shall watch
The canary bird will hear my song
Vanilla scent shall welcome my coming

Blow *Ijele* blow and let
Agbogomma see my colours
I have come to sing victory song
I have come to tell a victor's tale
Of long journey through thorny terrains
Of dark dank tunnel of torments
Through baptism of fire
To rite of passage to light

Now I will dance like *shaka*
I will growl like a victor lion
And prance like a jungle's panther
My plumage will outshine the peacock's
For I have climbed the *Iroko*
And removed its boastful crown
So I can now nod like the *Agama*
And walk with a royal gait
For I will sing my song of victory
And the big children will dance

Title: Towards the Aerial Plane
Medium: Coffee, dye and ink on paper
Year: 2000
Dimension: 17inches x 23inches.

EPILOGUE

The ability to harness elements from the visible and the verbal is one that stems from an analogous depth within human consciousness. This kinship between the two sister arts of poetry and painting have existed longer than can be imagined.

Practitioners in the field had long explored its greys and interconnectedness by transiting from one role to the other seamlessly. Lomazzo had observed that painting and poetry arrived at a single birth-differed. This is acknowledged in means and manner of expression, but are considered almost identical in fundamental nature in content and in purpose" (Rensselaer Lee.1998).

I get disappointed if my paintings are not exuding more of my desire to express textually and my writings are not revealing images of the myriad encounters, I find around my journey through life. Or maybe, my work, written or painted are not unconsciously exploring Ranciere's 'Sentence-image' concept through the depth of *Ut pictora poesis*.

Whatever is the situation, tracing the symbiosis of painting and poetry will surely locate a pristine quality in human expression through the text and image which I believe are coevals.

In my bid to write my experiences of life in text, image or even combination of all the faculties that nature provides, I may have been unable to write or paint faultlessly but my disposition has always been to write about my feelings on what is going on around me and also draw what my mind sees from my physical encounters. My natural desire is to create art (written or painted) through passion not subjected to the crucibles of commas, hyphen or grammatical ordering but to play with words and images exploring their emotive strength and turning experiences into play.

Most of the poems in this collection were written during school days in the University of Port Harcourt and University of Nigeria Nsukka (circa 1994 – 2001). The topics still find relevance today as most events have continued in character and depth hence art reaches the timeless issues of our societies.

ACKNOWLEDGEMENT

My song goes to Jehovah for my inspiration to sing in words and colours. Let him eternally be praised.

How do I express my gratitude to Doctor Ejine Okoroafor who provided a platform and reality? Thank you.

To Sinike and Chiazam, I owe a basketful of love and gratitude for those smiles that reveal more than they conceal.

My photo on the back cover credit goes to Carl Hazelwood.

The names of good people around me are legion. For exigencies of space and time, I say thank you all, as we look forward to understanding the secret behind the whispers of experience.